GET OUT OF THAT BOX

Unleash the Giant in You

NATALIE B. GREEN

GREEN HERITAGE
PUBLISHING

Copyright © 2018 by Natalie B. Green

All rights reserved. No part of this publication may be reproduced, stored in retrieval system, or transmitted in any form or by any means electronic, mechanical, photocopying, recording, or otherwise without prior written permission of the publisher.

Published by:
Green Heritage Publishing
3011 NW 175 Street
Miami Gardens, FL 33056

Unless otherwise noted, scripture quotations are taken from the King James Version of the Bible.
Public Domain

Get Out of That Box – Unleash the Giant in You
ISBN: 978-0-9600299-0-7

For Worldwide Distribution, Printed in the U.S.A.

Cover Design by Dee McIntosh
Logo Design by Christopher Thomas, PeculiarGFX
Front Cover Photo Credit: Lisa Durant – Durant Photography
Back Cover Photo Credit: Mark Hill Photography

www.nataliebgreen.com

DEDICATION

This book is dedicated to several people, whom God has used to awaken and unleash the giant in me.

To my husband and the love of my life, **James A. Green, Jr**. You shook me until I was awakened to the woman I was created to be. After all these years, your gentle nudges inspire me to be more, to look deeper and to go harder.

To my sweet **Melody**, my songbird, my muse. I do what I do mostly for you. I want to stir up the dreamer in you, babes. You will go further, achieve higher than I ever have. I'm in your corner, love, leading the fan club, putting the world on notice to stand up and pay attention; someone wonderful is on my heels.

To **Xavier**, my Nana-boy. At this tender age, my prayer is that you will follow my lead, son. You have in you everything you need to prosper and flourish. Fly high, baby-boy. There is NO limit!

To my siblings, **Shirley, Ruthie, Deborah, Vincent, Reginald, and Carolyn**. Each of you has inspired and empowered in some way. I am grateful for the part you have played in my journey. I couldn't walk through this life without you. Mandy

(Biscuit) taught us right. Her legacy still lives.

To **Althea Jackson,** I stood tall because I was standing on your shoulders. You took a chance on me and allowed me to shine. Thank you for sticking with me through my growing pains. I learned so much at your feet. I could never repay the debt I owe to you. I simply pray God will super-abundantly reward you in my stead.

To **Dr. Belinda John**, my twin in the Spirit. You looked inside me and said, "Natalie, come forth." God used you to give me a platform for my gift, and you motivated me to go for it and come out of hiding. My heart is forever yours.

SPECIAL TRIBUTE

Apostle Nina Marie Leslie

August 10, 1959 – October 22, 2018

I am grateful for this opportunity to pen a tribute to the phenomenal gift from Heaven, Apostle Nina Marie Leslie. There would be years between our passing but I am overwhelmed with honor to Father Dear for gracing me with a small space in your life and heart in your closing moments. Your aptness to love without limits and to give your heart and attention to the masses resounds as the anthem of your life. Your reach has spanned the boundaries of time and space and flooded the hearts of many with assurance and hope.

It's hard to imagine that even while you were in an unfavorable condition in your body, your heart pushed you to read my book and send me uplifting words of encouragement. Your presence in this realm has left a void that only Holy Spirit can fill, but your impact has left an indelible mark on my heart. It is my prayer dear sister that at the peak of my journey, I find myself to have emulated your great love for all of God's creation. You lived well and loved greatly. You will be forever in my heart as I press forward and upward in great anticipation that I will see you again.

All my love,

Natalie

Acknowledgments

Heart of God Ministries Church Family

Pastors Roy and Louise McFadden – Seedtime and Harvest Faith Ministry

Pastor Michael and Apostle Kimberly Holmes – Healing House Ministries

Pastors Anthony and Shantel Accilien – Christ World Prayer Center

Pastors Tommie and Colleen Collins – Spirit of Deliverance Church

Pastors Tony and Deborah Kemp – Tony Kemp Ministries

Erania Witherspoon – Soul-Lifted Sisters Prayer Ministry

Secoya Parker-Jones – Midwife, Entrepreneur, Speaker

Lakeisha Dixon – The Breakthrough Strategist

Charles and Rhonda Johnson

Dr. Emile and Lisa Hawkins

TABLE OF CONTENTS

Introduction 1

Chapter 1: Jack and Jill Get out of That Box 5

Chapter 2: Move to the Beat of Your Destiny 9

Chapter 3: Change Your Self Talk 13

Chapter 4: Silence the Ground Noise 17

Chapter 5: Fail Forward 21

Chapter 6: Invest in You – You Are Worth It 25

Chapter 7: Fire the Packers and Stay Free 29

Chapter 8: What Is No? 35

Chapter 9: Pop Already! 39

Chapter 10: For Leading Ladies Only 45

Chapter 11: Change Happens When Change Happens
(Affirmation) 49

Conclusion: The End from the Beginning 53

About the Author 57

Contact 59

Introduction

The fact that you are reading this book is an indication that you are destined to win. The sound of your destiny is calling, and you've embarked upon a journey to break free from the excuses that have held you in confinement.

Being held back in any manner when the beckoning sound of your best self is ringing in your ears is like having an itch that you can't scratch. At some point, desperation kicks in, and sparks of creativity and innovation begin to awaken in you—thus jumpstarting your quest to defy the odds and refute the status quo just to discover a way to scratch that itch.

There are times when I consider myself a late bloomer. I was married at the tender age of twenty-one. My heart was flooded with dreams of the perfect life far from the limitations of my early childhood. I just knew that I was destined to be something wonderful and that marrying James A. Green—a gifted man and a minister who adored me—would lead to the introduction of Natalie the Great.

Somehow I believed that all the fear and timidity I had would magically disappear because I was married to this man who was the exact opposite of who I was. I took comfort in the idea that I could simply hide behind his bold and powerful persona and thereby camouflage my personal fears and inner conflict. This was my opportunity to escape the images of lack and desperation that were common scenery in my life. Perhaps now I could be like *"those people"* by whom I'd measured my own success. I could have what they have and forget about the woes of yesteryear.

Needless to say, life happened! Life has a way of taking you on a track that is as far from your plan as the east is from the west. We experienced some level of success here and there, but it was nothing like I thought it would be. I was still miserable. I seemed to be living outside my body, going through the motions of life but never really living. We were both intelligent people but had no idea what we were doing. We had not been taught how to manage money or been coached on how to create the life we wanted to live with our God-given gifts. We just trekked through life stabbing at the darkness, hoping to hit that moment that would be our turning point.

My husband finally landed his dream job, which kept him away from home a lot. Did I say a lot? There I was, with nothing but time on my hands to think about how empty I was. I had no vision for my life. I had become comfortable hiding in his shadow, but now something (destiny) from deep within me began to call again.

My husband, a very intuitive man, saw how miserable I had

become and would often ask me, what do you want to do with your life, or what do you dream of becoming? I remember so vividly answering him out of my fear to venture beyond his shadow, "I just want to support you, babe." His wisdom would not allow him to take that answer at face value. He periodically came back to me with his query as well as encouragement for me to GET A LIFE.

Well, in our tenth year of marriage, I started my first business. Very quickly I discovered I really had something of value to offer. My business took off; I began to service large corporations and millionaire clientele in my event planning company. I was alive! In the fifth year of that business, I was able to walk away from my eighteen-year job in a non-profit agency where I had become Assistant Director to do events full time.

My first business was the catalyst I needed to shift my mindset to a true understanding of what was really buried inside of me. My fear kept me confined to hiding in the shadows when I was created to stand in the spotlight. Since that time, I have definitely experienced some challenging times, but instead of hiding, I turn up the temperature of my desire to be my best self, and I keep it moving.

The release of this first book comes at a turning point in my life. I'm 54 and just really beginning to live again. What I have learned over all these years is that there are many firsts. We get the opportunity to experience rebirth after rebirth as we relentlessly take the journey to discover all that has been placed on the inside of us. Am I a late bloomer? Maybe. There are many new beginnings awaiting us as long as we are willing to keep exploring. No need to stop at the peak of one mountain; there are many more mountains daring us to conquer them.

Some people live their entire lives never connecting with the sound of their destiny. So many have had their unrealized potential for greatness carefully tucked away in a box and sealed with packing tape marked "fragile—handle with care." Congratulations, my friend. It could have been you, but it isn't. From the very moment you picked up this book, the universe was set in motion to make room for its next Mover, Shaker, and Dominator.

This book will provoke the desperation in you to scratch that itch! You will begin to discover your own uniqueness as well as be empowered to burst loose, break the tape, and pop the weasel to demolish the cycles of negative thinking that have held you at bay. Walls and ceilings of containment are already starting to rumble. Can you hear it? It's your time, your season, and your moment to get out of that box and unleash the giant in you.

~ CHAPTER 1 ~

Jack and Jill Get out of That Box

Do you remember playing with that all too familiar toy as a child called a Jack-in-the-box? Its intrigue was two-fold: the clanky tune that sounded as the handle was turned, along with the surprise of this clown-dressed doll (the Weasel) popping up, seemingly on a whim.

What we could not understand as a child was that, as long as the right sound played, the Weasel was programmed to pop out of that box. I gathered some interesting thoughts from observing this long forgotten child's toy, which so clearly imitates certain real-life circumstances.

For one thing, I liken the sound that causes Jack the Weasel to pop up from the box to the sound of destiny's call. There is no life to be lived confined in a box. Next, I realized that both the speed and rhythm of the sound are controlled by an operator residing outside of the box. That idea spoke loudly to me and assured me that if we surrender to the will and work of the "Master Operator," sooner or later, we will pop out. One person's time to pop out may be different from someone else's, but the potential to pop is encoded in our DNA. The thought of that should diffuse any competition with each other because we are all destined to get our turn.

I find that the greatest pleasure is experienced when the reveal takes place. The anticipation to see what's inside is at last fulfilled when what is hidden away in obscurity is set free. One final observation I'd like to point out is that those who flourish in their experience of freedom outside of the box are oftentimes squeezed, mashed, and stuffed right back inside. Not everyone you encounter will be equipped to handle who you are destined to be; therefore, they attempt to trap and imprison you in the confines of their own vision and opinion of who you are.

There are countless processes in life that could stifle our efforts to become who we are really meant to be—social status, educational and cultural barriers, historical and generational mindsets, self-doubt, and fear to name a few. This writer believes that every single living soul who is allowed to pass through the Earth in space and time are obligated, by their mere existence, to leave a deposit of their own uniqueness in the world.

Each person's individual giftedness is as distinctive as a fingerprint, but it is all supposed to work in symphony with the distinctiveness of others in a particular sphere of influence. The question then becomes, what happens to the community where so many parts are undiscovered and unexpressed? The answer: Where there should be beautiful, melodic tones and breathtaking harmonies, there is only indistinguishable and chaotic

NOISE.

I realize it may be a difficult thing to imagine that your little part in the great expanse of the universe could make any difference at all. However, our individual part set in motion as we become alive to our authentic selves makes an impact in small drops right where we are then reverberates throughout our families, community and ultimately the world. We cannot allow ourselves to focus only on the big picture when we have not become congnizant of how much power we possess to make a difference right where we are.

The point I desire to convey is that we have to start where we are. We cannot afford to spend one more moment living an aimless – unintentional life. The generations that are rising quickly upon our heels are in desperate need of positive, yet familiar examples of what a life in its fullness looks like. It is our duty to participate in the symphony of life and create a sound that will perpetuate good in the earth. It starts with each one of us getting out of the box and becoming present.

Let's Go Deeper

What is the name of your box?

Take a moment to identify and name the things that have kept you from being free

~ CHAPTER 2 ~

Move to the Beat of Your Destiny

It is very easy to follow the crowd as we move through life. No creativity or thoughtfulness is needed if you're just going to go with the flow to which you have become accustomed. There are certain characteristics we develop as we live life in a particular culture. Our personalities, preferences, and tendencies are largely a result of the norms, habits, and practices of those in and around our community. We take upon us particles from the environment in which we live.

It is quite common to see people dressing, acting, and living in a similar manner simply because they reside in the same environment. For posterity's sake, this could be a good thing; however, when the person you were created to be conflicts with the norms of your environment, you must make the critical decision to get out of the box of routine and tradition in order to break free.

There is a distinct sound and beat written in your DNA, which will direct you to paths that lead to the fulfillment of your destiny. For many, that sound or that beat can only be heard by the bearer. As a result, conflict may arise between family members, friends, and others because one person decided to break rank and move to the beat of their own destiny. How many times have you heard of stories where parents and children are at odds with one another because the family had one plan for the child but the child went in a completely opposite direction?

Perhaps the expectation of the father was for the son to take over the family business and continue a legacy passed down from generation to generation. However, when the time comes, the child decides to do something that has never before been done in the family bloodline. That person is moving to the beat of his own destiny.

The truth of the matter is, once a person hears and acknowledges his/her own unique call to destiny, anything less will only cause them to live a miserable existence. Destiny and purpose are the cornerstones upon which to build a free and enjoyable life. I am reminded of the insightful words spoken by my daughter Melody one day, as we held a discussion along these lines. She said, *"Life without purpose is no life at all."*

How enlightening and profound a statement coming from someone who has, for her entire life, moved to the beat of her own destiny. She understood at an early age that living YOUR life was the only life to live.

Let's Go Deeper

What is the sound of your destiny calling you to become?

Write about the road you are currently on and determine if it will lead you to fulfill your destiny

_____

_____

_____

_____

_____

_____

_____

_____

_____

_____

_____

_____

_____

"'Unleash Me!' Are the words that came out of my mouth in the first chapter! Natalie is the guru of motivation and mental shift. She writes with so much revelation and with revelation the picture is painted in the canvas of your mind. I am a GIANT. I was born to live outside the box. This book will fuel your inspiration for more. You will thirst for your destiny with a sense of urgency.

"These strategies will catapult you into living your best life starting today. It's Time To Step Into Your Destiny! It's Time To Get Out The Box! It's Time To Step Into Greatness! It's Time To Win!"

Lakeisha Dixon - The Breakthrough Strategies

~ CHAPTER 3 ~

Change Your Self Talk

I have been privileged to spend a lot of time engaging with people from various walks of life in the capacity of mentor, coach, counselor, confidant, and friend. As I operated in one or more of these capacities, I have discovered that negative self-talk is a notorious enemy to the forward progress of any person.

I have encountered many people who build personal prisons because of the negative words they speak, both consciously and unconsciously, to themselves. The culprit behind these negative narratives stems from one's own perspective of self-worth and value gathered from a history of programming by negative influences in their lives. The way a person views themself is often based upon someone else's valuation of them. For example, a child who is raised in a home that lacks positive affirmation, encouragement, and honor oftentimes grows up believing they have very little value. This reality is common amongst persons from dysfunctional family structures, as well as for persons who associate themselves with people who are victims of the same negative culture.

Such a person is in desperate need of a "mind dump." A mind dump is what I call the process of replacing negative thoughts, understandings, and beliefs with positive and affirmative thoughts, which increase one's sense of self-worth. The Bible calls it being transformed by the renewing of the mind in Romans 12:1-2. We've heard for many years that your mouth speaks from the abundance of your heart. If all you have in your heart and mind is junk, then you are destined to think junk thoughts, speak junk words and live a junk life.

Remember the cliché "you are what you eat"? Thinking this way will help you understand the importance of guarding what you allow your eyes to see and ears to hear concerning your identity and self-worth. If you are going to get out of that box, YOU must make a decision to digest and speak only words and concepts that build your character and fortify your sense of self-respect, confidence, and pride. In some cases, drastic measures must be employed to protect yourself from toxic environments.

There is a young man I've known for many years who grew up in what we could call a toxic environment. As far as he could see, there was one person after another walking through life with no vision, no expectation, and no success in any area of life. Poverty, sickness, fear, and depression were a few of the dangerous behaviors he witnessed repeat themselves over and over again. He was a very intelligent young man who understood that what he witnessed around him could spread like an airborne infection, with the potency to kill any dream he had of going further in life than what he was used to seeing.

Finding himself in this predicament as a young teen, he made the drastic decision to leave his parents' home in order to recalibrate his life. He had to change what he saw and heard to enable him to speak the life-giving words to himself. This young man had dreams that would have died had he remained in such a toxic environment. I'm sure everyone would call this a bold and risky move, but this young man had two choices: he could remain where he was and become a dead man walking, or he could take the difficult shot and really live. I am proud to say, that young man is now a full-grown entrepreneur, with several streams of income and living a full, happy, and healthy life. He changed what he ate in order to change what he'd become.

Let's Go Deeper

Think about what you're thinking about

Make a list of new thoughts you will begin to speak to yourself

_____

_____

_____

_____

_____

_____

_____

_____

_____

_____

_____

_____

~ CHAPTER 4 ~

Silence the Ground Noise

It is sometimes easier to go through life unconcerned about where you will end up. One could easily submit to another person's destination label, as opposed to reaching beyond pre-determined limits and living one's highest and best life.

The primary use of a label on the outside of a box is to set the destination of the package, but there is also something inside the box called a packing slip. A packing slip is a list of quantities and descriptions of what is on the inside of the box. Common descriptions may include comfort, complacency, mediocrity, familiarity, just getting by, nothing special, or loser. I think you get the idea.

No matter what word is used, to a person who understands who and what they were created to be, it's just ground noise. As you progress in your ascent, you will come to a crossroads requiring you to choose whether to conform to a pre-described destination or to identify with the description on the packing slip created by others. The greatest decision you could ever make in this case is to silence the ground noise and push harder and higher in pursuit of the freedom that is rightfully yours.

Ground noise is often a result of fear, self-doubt, and lack of clarity regarding your true identity as prescribed to you by the Creator, Himself. I recall an account in scripture (Jeremiah 1:4-8) when God unveiled His purpose to the Prophet Jeremiah. Immediately, Jeremiah responded with words stemming from the ground noise of self-doubt and inadequacy. Unfortunately, too many people forfeit their ability to walk fully into purpose because they have not gained clarity from their Creator about who they are meant to be. Instead, they live life in a confined space, made captive by their own misconceptions.

The thing about ground noise is that the higher you rise, the weaker its volume and the less significant its effect. We spoke in the previous chapter about self-talk. When ground noise is released in your hearing, you have to immediately employ evasive maneuvers. You cannot afford to spend one second considering ground noise as your truth. At that critical moment, you must begin to override the penetrating effects of the ground noise by speaking to yourself OUT LOUD. Begin to speak those things you have discovered to be in line with keeping you free.

Friend, the cemetery is overflowing with unrealized dreams, aspirations, and potential. Countless persons have lived insignificant lives but died monumental deaths because they have carried everything God put in them back to the grave. Let us choose to live a monumental life and leave this Earth emptied out.

Let's Go Deeper

Formulate your evasive maneuvers

Plan how you will accomplish your goals no matter what anyone else says

_____

_____

_____

_____

_____

_____

_____

_____

_____

_____

_____

_____

"*GET OUT OF THAT BOX* is a work of inspiration, revelation and motivation! As a masterful storyteller, she lays out the process one may walk through in order to overcome obstacles, to turn potential into possibility and God's revelation into a personal reality.

"The revelations that Natalie shares through the Holy Spirit, build a bridge that one may cross over by planning, prayer and persistence into divine destiny!!! If a person applies what they read, they can change their world by the revelation of the Word and the person of the Holy Spirit!"

Pastor Tony Kemp - Tony Kemp Ministries

~ CHAPTER 5 ~

Fail Forward

The thought of failing in any direction is likely a terrifying idea for most people. However, my desire is to provoke you to think differently about failure. Everything you encounter in life has the ability to bury you or produce newness in you. Failure is no different.

As you reach toward becoming truly free, some of the strategies you employ to aid you may not work as well as you had hoped. You may fail more than once, twice, or even a hundred times, but there is good news. Failing forward means your failure is not the end of your hope; instead, it becomes the channel from which creative ideas, new insights, greater understanding, and practical experience is birthed.

Perspective is everything! In your journey to breaking free, you are going to have to change your perspective on much of what you've been taught to believe. Once you adopt the failing forward perspective, the chains of fear and self-doubt will crumble. The freedom you receive in this process will enable you to do what you've never done as well as achieve what you never have before.

All failure is not created equal. There are times when failure is the instrument used to highlight personal vulnerabilities and character defects. In that sense, failure has become a flag of warning or an indicator that development is needed in order to ensure that the success we strive for will stand strong through the inevitable storms of life. The worst thing a person can do is reach a pinnacle of success by their giftedness only to crash and burn because their character and inner strength were insufficient to sustain them there.

There is a man in scripture, in the book of Exodus, named Moses. His name means "to draw out" or "deliverer". Although he was taken away from his family and raised in the house of the enemy, the older he got the louder the sound of destiny rang out in his heart. As the story goes, it was that call, which moved him to deliver his kinsmen from a slave-driver. Needless to say, this attempt to answer the call of his destiny was an epic failure. His failure led him to become a murderer and fugitive from justice.

This failure was not Moses' finest hour, but neither was it the end of his story. Moses fails at his first attempt, but he failed forward. His failure led him to the back side of the desert where he was stripped of self-reliance, the residue of a false identity, as well as taming his quick-fire temper.

Yes, he found himself boxed in on the back side of the desert, but destiny found him there, and he became the deliverer he was created to be. What's the takeaway? You may fail—just be sure to fail forward. Get up and try it again. Make the necessary adjustments, then try it again and again until something breaks.

Let's Go Deeper

Did you really fail or did you just get a fresh start?

Think about the times you've failed and what you can use as fuel to succeed in the future

_____
_____
_____
_____
_____
_____
_____
_____
_____
_____
_____
_____
_____

"I am so blown away, I am trying to recapture my running mind & slow down my thoughts of speed! I feel like this writing is infused with quantum properties. I feel like it gushed out of you so quickly & adroitly, that maybe you don't even realize the strength of what you are postured to release. I feel like Brother Man ... I am a man undone!

"This writing slays me, over and over again. Feel like I have to come up for air, just to not drown in the water. Ham mercy! I will take a day or so break from this writing, then read it again. I am in such marvel of our God, who would place so much of Him in you!"

Apostle Nina Marie Leslie, Founder and Sr. Visionary

Speaking The Word Only Ministries, Inc.

~ CHAPTER 6 ~

Invest in You – You Are Worth It

The thought of investing in oneself is a difficult notion for some to take hold of—especially those of us who spend our entire existence promoting the success of others. We will support mission projects in our church and community efforts for the less fortunate. We are the supermoms for our children and cheerleaders for our spouses—all the while forgetting to tuck a little of that loving support away for ourselves.

I have come across people who actually harbor feelings of guilt and condemnation because they took some time to treat themselves in a special way or, heaven forbid, say no to someone. Much of this behavior stems from a place of low self-worth and inferiority, which we addressed briefly in Chapter 3. It's as if that person feels fully alive only if they are pouring out of themselves to others, but beware. There is danger in constantly giving out of the treasures of our hearts without taking the time to get poured back into.

Though you are a spirit at your core, you are also body and soul. In order to live the successful life you want spiritually, physically, mentally, and financially, you must habitually and purposefully position yourself to be elevated as well as replenished. Invest in yourself! Much profit is made by the person who recognizes their need to grow. The more you know, the better the edge you will have in a particular sphere of influence. It is very important that you keep your fingers on the pulse of changes and new discoveries in your field of expertise.

Everything you need to prosper was embedded into your DNA as a seed, but you have to be adamant about building that seed and increasing that seed to the point that you can thrive and prosper. Otherwise, you will watch those into whom you have invested continue to rise and conquer while you are empty and pitiful. It is the truth you know that will make you free and keep you out of the box of fatigue, exhaustion, and depletion.

A good example of investing in yourself is enrolling in classes to increase your knowledge base, join a Bible study, or hire a coach who will challenge you and provoke you to flourish personally. Networking with those who are beyond the level you are on is a wonderful way to introduce a new hunger within you. You cannot run around the yard with chickens your entire life. At some point, you are going to have to start rubbing shoulders with some eagles.

Yes! Doing the things I suggest may cost you some money, but not doing them may cost you everything. Remember, your goal is to live a monumental life, not die a monumental death.

Let's Go Deeper

It's time to increase your personal portfolio

List the new things you will invest in yourself

_____

_____

_____

_____

_____

_____

_____

_____

_____

_____

_____

_____

~ CHAPTER 7 ~

Fire the Packers and Stay Free

I recall the season in my life when at last, my journey to self-discovery paid off. I finally knew who I was and what I was destined to become. I was full of excitement and elation as I plotted my trail to become fully alive. I expected the entire universe to rejoice with me, but unfortunately, that was not the case. In fact, as I plotted, trained, and invested time and attention into my newly discovered awareness—life happened.

It seemed adverse circumstances and situations rose up on every side. Everything demanded my attention at the most inopportune time. I mean, I simply had no headspace to deal with one more issue. These things seemed to be on a mission to prevent me from becoming the person I knew I was supposed to be. Everything that happened sought to keep me distracted and overwhelmed so I'd give up and return to my confined space beneath bubble wrap, submerged in a sealed box.

In my distress, I remember praying and crying out to God from the depths of my soul for help. My heart was overwhelmed with fear that everything I'd gained was about to be lost. In the midst of that emotional turmoil, help arrived. In an enlightened moment, I remembered that I had power over the narratives that were bombarding my thoughts. After all, my own words have the greatest influence in my life, so, I began to say out loud, "**But I know who I am, I know who I am.**"

Whew! Talk about a come to Jesus moment! I knew then I could not go back to the way it used to be. In fact, I realized that who I really was could no longer fit in the box from which I had been liberated. I had been a GIANT in a box, and no matter what came my way, I was never going to be imprisoned again.

This became a crossroads for me. I made a decision that day to Fire the Packers! The packers—i.e., *negative thoughts, fear, and hopelessness*—offered me only the comfort of familiarity. After all, we'd spent a lot of time together through the years, and we knew what to expect from each other. Still, the taste of freedom I'd experienced outside the box made me hungry for more. Instead of succumbing to the enticements of the familiar place, I chose to adjust my focus, release what was beyond my control to God, and keep making steps towards exploring the new freedoms that awaited me.

As you continue on your journey, you will discover that staying free is not a one and done occurrence. Everything you do from this point on must be done intentionally and purposefully, to overcome any and all threats to your freedom. An understanding of the power of well-placed boundaries will afford you a tremendous advantage over the packer's influence. Packers use bubble wrap as a cushion as well as to hold you tightly in place; the closer you are to the familiar, the more comfortable and non-resistant you will become.

Therefore, a change in focus is critical to your pursuit of true freedom. Focusing only on the closest thing to you will never ignite a desire for more. Your focus is fueled by your deepest hunger, but if you never step outside of the familiar place and explore beyond the borders of complacency, your appetite for what awaits you will not be awakened. Genesis 5:3-5 (NKJV) gives us a glimpse into what I wish to convey.

³ *Then Abram said, "Look, You have given me no offspring; indeed one born in my house is my heir!"* ⁴ *And behold, the word of the* LORD *came* to him, saying, *"This one shall not be your heir, but one who will come* **from your own body** *shall be your heir."* ⁵ *Then* **He brought him outside** *and said, "Look now toward heaven, and count the stars if you are able to number them." And He said to him, "So shall your descendants be."*

The Patriarch, Abram experienced a shift in his focus only after God brought him out of his tent (box). Although Abram had made great progress toward fulfilling his destiny, the words of the packers along with the way he saw himself haunted him. He accepted the word of the packers and thought that what he had was all he'd ever have relating to an heir. In fact, he had already begun to formulate a *plan B* because in his mind he no longer had what it took to produce the very thing he was created for.

Abram had **tent vision** so God brought him out of that limited place and commanded him to look beyond where he was. He had to change what he was looking at in order to change what he would receive. Following this encounter, there was no turning back for Abram. A shift in focus produced a shift in his belief and facilitated the manifestation of his true purpose. Genesis 15:6 says *"And he believed in the LORD…"*

Your freedom will always be under attack. The packers will never celebrate your victories but will keep coming back with new ways to imprison you again. Use your progress as a source of inspiration to remain free and fully alive, no matter what.

Let's Go Deeper

You're Fired!

Make a list of who or what you will let go of in order to remain Free

_____
_____
_____
_____
_____
_____
_____
_____
_____
_____
_____
_____

"The book, GET OUT OF THAT BOX, by Natalie Green is not only a phenomenal work, but it is a compelling thrust of potent prescriptions of thought for anyone looking to engage, not just exist in the places of purpose and destiny. As an avid reader, I come across many books that promise to empower and engage, but they don't quite deliver the life lessons in a way that anyone who reads it can understand.

"After reading this masterful piece of collective thoughts, principles, and anecdotes, it is clear that Natalie Green is not only a prolific writer, but an experienced mentor that knows how to inspire and coach you through the scribe's pen. Natalie's words spoke to the core of my thinking as well as inspired the passion of my heart. Get out of that Box is a must read."

Dr. Ursula T. Wright, Founder

Disruption Movement

~ CHAPTER 8 ~

What Is No?

If you are reading this book, I believe that NO is a word, an attitude, or a paradigm with which you are acquainted. It is a force that equips the user with the power to win when all the odds are against them. How can a word comprised of only two letters be so potent? "No" is more than just a word; it is, in many instances, a mindset, oftentimes passed down from generation to generation.

NO has been the warden keeping you captive in the land that confines your purpose and kills your courage. Those two letters have sealed the fate of untold numbers in boxes, prisons, toxic relationships, and environments.

This two-letter word has been found guilty and convicted in the courts of life as a thief of destinies, a murderer of dreams, and a destroyer of potential. Many aspiring individuals have succumbed to the devastating effects of "No". They have simply given up on ever unleashing the giant that roars from deep within them. So many have settled for destitution rather than starting a revolution that could release them into the life they were created to live.

A just-getting-by and can-hardly-get-along reality is not what you and I were created for, my friend! At this point in our journey, we must grasp the understanding that anything worth having is worth fighting for. You have got to allow the giant spirit that has been locked securely away inside you to put the universe on notice. Make up in your mind today—I said *today*—that you are getting out, staying out, and showing out.

You have a God-given right to be free. A high cost has been paid for your freedom. We were all judged guilty and sentenced to death, but by His mercy, God used the power of no to redeem us back to Himself. God looks at you and me and says, you are worth it.

Now it's your turn. It's about time you employed the power of NO. *No* to bondage, *No* to lack, *No* to abuse, *No* to the glass ceiling, *No* to negativity, and *No* to unrealized dreams. What is NO? It is the power you need to stand through opposition, overcome obstacles, flip the script, quench darts of doubt and fear, and it is the power you need to live a monumental life outside of that box!

Let's Go Deeper

Turn No into an Ally instead of an Enemy

List the steps you will take to use the power of NO to your advantage

_____

_____

_____

_____

_____

_____

_____

_____

_____

_____

_____

_____

"Are you ready to throw caution to the wind, then ride the wind to your place of authentic freedom? This would be a good place to say out loud, 'I'm getting out of that box!'"

~ CHAPTER 9 ~

Pop Already!

It is my sincere desire that at this point in our journey, your eyes have been opened and you actually see the giant you have the potential to be. It's not enough to come all this way and still remain in the same conditions as you were before we began. I recently had a dream that has really spoken volumes to me as it relates to living a purposeful and free life.

In the dream, many plans had been made toward conducting a seminar or empowerment conference. Many people from all walks of life were registered and waiting with great anticipation for this opportunity. Suddenly, everything came to a screeching halt! The host decided it was not worth it. They had no idea of the anticipation surrounding their planned event. I so vividly remember the shock and confusion on the face of those doctors, nurses, influencers, and other professionals when they found out that the event had been canceled.

This group was so hungry for what this person had to give that they hurried about trying to do whatever it took to accommodate the host and the event. I dream a lot, but rarely can I remember so vividly what the dreams were about. I believe I am able to recall this dream so well because it carries such a powerful underlying message. It expressed to me the importance of us popping up when the sound of destiny is released.

That dream showed me how so many are waiting with bated breath for what we have. It also showed me the devastation that takes place every time someone's sound of destiny is ignored and a person refuses to pop out of the place of obscurity. Dear heart, this is no time for lurking in the shadows of fear and self-doubt. There are people waiting for you to pop.

You were born with a unique gift that is intended to impact a particular population. Somebody needs what you have in order to kindle the fires of purpose and destiny buried within them. You hold the missing puzzle piece to someone's hopes and dreams becoming a reality; it is just the order of things. Are you willing to risk it all? Will you accept the assignment to be a world shaker and dominator? Have you had enough of an insignificant life? If your answer is yes, then Pop Already!

It's too late for me. I've tasted the sweetness of freedom. The question is, are you hungry enough to do what it takes? Are you ready to throw caution to the wind, then ride the wind to your place of authentic freedom? This would be a good place to say out loud, "I'm getting out of that box!"

There was a time in my life when I felt like nothing more than the walking dead, a mere skeleton of a person. I had cast away all hopes of ever knowing what it would feel like to live a full, happy life. As a result, I poured whatever I had left into the lives of anyone who could make use of the "little" I had to offer. An empty shell, I found myself grasping at some sense of fulfillment in the accomplishments of others.

To my surprise, pouring into others unveiled a hidden truth; I finally understood that there was more in me than I had imagined. Once I was awakened to the giant potential inside of me, I embarked on a journey to come out of the deep, dark box that held me captive for far too long.

Coming out of that place was a delicate process. Who I was authentically could become a lifestyle threat for those into whom I'd poured. You see, now I was drinking from the fountain, which had only provided sustenance to others.

My prayers sustained me through many sleepless nights as I traversed the road to freedom. The pressure to go back to being the person I was is always lurking in the shadows, with chains in tow. However, in every encounter with the ghosts of yesterday's bondage, I renew my decision to be authentically me.

I have perpetually resolved that no matter the cost, or how thunderous the screams of bondage are, I WILL NOT get back in that box again. I am **Unboxed and Dangerous!** The world may not be ready for me, but I am most assuredly ready for it! Does this sound like where you are right now? Say it out loud, **I am Unboxed and Dangerous!**

"This book is a clear example of John 8:32: And you shall know the truth, and the truth shall make you free. I say this because Natalie's courage to be transparent about her life, starting with the introduction will give the reader the courage to face their truth without condemnation; therefore, causing them to get out the box of their life and step right into the freedom to live the life they desire."

Prophetess Colleen Collins, Co-Pastor

Spirit of Deliverance Ministries

Let's Go Deeper

The Power to be Free is in your hands

Write about what you will do from this moment to get out and stay out of That Box

_____

_____

_____

_____

_____

_____

_____

_____

_____

_____

_____

_____

_____

_____

"I hope by sharing a real piece of my journey that you, my sister, will know beyond any doubt that you can do this. In the words of the old church mother, 'I have found Him to be a keeper.'"

~ CHAPTER 10 ~

For Leading Ladies Only

I magine with me for a moment that this book is actually a fairly large social event where many of the Who's Who are gathered. There you are, working the room, shoulder-to-shoulder with VIPs and Socialites. On the surface, you may be the life of the party, but underneath the veneer of a self-made powerhouse, what you really want is for someone to come to you and say, "Would you like to step outside and get some air?"

Well, I'm your good BFF today, and I'm asking you to join me for a breath of fresh air. See, I know the real you. I know what you really want is for someone to assure you that they understand what it really costs to be you. In your current existence, the sacrifices you make to be this phenomenal Leading Lady everyone is reaching for may never be revealed. My desire in this chapter is to make you aware of this one thing: you are not alone.

I realize this may not be the reality of everyone reading this book, but it is an everyday truth for so many of us. I want you to take a moment to just breathe. Block out the noise of your heels clanging on the floor as you rush from the boardroom, the meet-and-greet mixer, or the power lunch, and just breathe. Be encouraged, my sister. You've come so far and accomplished so much, and yet you reach for more. I applaud you, and I celebrate you.

I pray you will take this moment to rediscover the little girl inside of you who is now buried beneath the mass of accolades, degrees, and achievements. Think about that little girl who, in simpler times, dreamed of becoming something wonderful when she grew up—the time when the word **impossible** was a defeated foe in the face of her fearless resolve.

Sometimes, to break free from the entanglements that are standard as a person is elevated, you just need to take time to remember. Revisit your personal philosophy, which was initially founded upon a deep desire to make a difference. You see, I have found that true feelings of joy and fulfillment have been at their highest when I was making a difference in someone else's life. However, success has a way of redefining our missions and reshaping our dreams to the point that we wake up one morning and find that we have forgotten why we started doing what we were doing in the first place.

I have a special place in my heart for ladies in ministry because I am one. I can identify with the struggle of having the right look, the right style, the right skill, and so on. The load we carry as women in ministry, as first ladies, co-pastors, and the like can often be overwhelming. It seems we are held to unrealistic standards with little room for flexibility.

On-lookers find it hard to believe the loneliness we experience, even in the midst of packed houses and sold out conferences. The fear of being exposed as *"normal"* haunts us. The thought of something going awry in our efforts can be intimidating and downright scary. Take comfort, my sister. Your Father's love will ever abound toward you. He is quite comfortable with you revealing your cosmetic-free face, ragged comfy sweats, and not-so-perfect hairstyle to Him in your moments of quiet desperation. In fact, He longs for those moments where there is only you and Him, for it is in those moments that we receive refreshing and replenishment.

Allow me to share a transparent moment with you. The following is a snippet of an entry I made in one of my journals written some years ago, but every time I revisit it, the emotional force that was present when I wrote it comes rushing in. Better yet, a solemn praise rises up within me because it also reminds me of how good God is to me and from how far He has brought me.

<u>Never thought I'd cry these tears again (8/2/2014)</u>

"… I am so broken right now I can barely stand to get out of the bed again. The all too familiar pain of yesterday comes rushing in with the piercing rays of each new day's sun. What am I to do? I've opened the gate to my heart only to realize too late that it was bound to be broken again. There's so much to consider now; I have no strategy for dealing with this. Life is topsy-turvy, and I don't know which way is up.

"That Pain in the pit of my stomach keeps me tossing and turning with uncertainty—a by-product of my need to internalize my brokenness in order to preserve my image as a 'strong Christian woman.' All the while I am a little child with up-stretched arms begging to be picked up by someone bigger and stronger than I.

"What am I to do when the harsh winds of disappointment are blowing in from every side? Seems I have to scrape through every accomplishment on my belly to escape the wires only inches above my head that are designed to keep me confined.

"This box seems to get smaller and smaller every day while my hopes and aspirations continue to grow. Seems I'm about to reach critical mass and something is about to break. Am I prepared? Am I strong enough to survive? Will the day come that I can look back on this season and smile? I can only hope.

"It's not enough for me to preach a good message; I need to live the message I preach. If people only knew the fountain from which their thirst is quenched is bone dry... I have nothing left."

I hope by sharing a *real* piece of my journey that you, my sister, will know beyond any doubt that you can do this. In the words of the old church mother, I have found Him to be a keeper. Be assured, my sister, you are not forgotten, neither are you alone. There are multiplied thousands of us building a united front on the frontlines, in our homes, our neighborhoods, and in our churches. God's Leading Ladies are on the rise; we're getting out of the box and breaking free of everything that held us captive.

~ CHAPTER 11 ~

Change Happens When Change Happens (Affirmation)

You are genetically empowered to create. God framed the world by the Word of His power (Hebrew 11:3), and He has given you the power to do the same.

Your world is voice-activated, and your voice has the power to shift atmospheres as well as change the world you see. Set aside some time each day to reinforce the foundation of your newly found truth with these Change Happens affirmations. Say these out loud with conviction:

Because change happens when change happens…

- I speak from my spirit and declare TRUTH to my mind and body.

- I declare that today is a new beginning in my life. The person I was yesterday no longer exists. I Am Changed!

- Everything I do from this moment on will be in alignment with my Divine purpose.

- I will renew my mind and change my world by what I say.

- I will live inside out! I will change my routine and walk in the spirit and put to death the cravings and negative tendencies of my flesh.

- I will change my appetite. I will no longer eat on low levels but will eat the things that produce strength, growth, and maturity in me.

- I will remove myself from relationships that contribute to my immaturity.

- I will change what I see. I will expand my sights beyond where I am to where I am going.

- I will make connections that empower me for greatness.

- I was created with dominion power, and I will take authority.

- I will be a person of integrity and good character.

- I will attract favor and goodwill in every sphere of life.

- I refuse to be satisfied with what is and what was. I will dream bigger dreams, reach higher heights, and conquer new mountains.

- I will transition with ease through every terrain I encounter.

GET OUT OF THAT BOX

- I will feed my gift with wisdom, knowledge, and understanding.

- I have within me the power to prosper in every area of life.

- Everything I touch will prosper, grow, and expand.

- I will use my resources to be an agent of goodwill to others.

- I will be an extravagant and cheerful giver.

- I will be a confident, bold, fearless warrior.

- I Am a Game-Changer and a Giant-Slayer because nothing is impossible for me.

- I was born for this! I am unmovable, unshakable, unstoppable, and free.

- I Will Never get in that box again!

Let's Go Deeper

Write some affirmations of your own

Think about what you want your life to look like and declare it.

CONCLUSION

The End from the Beginning

The foundation upon which this work is established reaches deep into the origin of mankind. The Bible says, in Genesis 2:26, 28 that God created mankind in His image and likeness, and that mankind was created to have dominion. We were not to be dominated or imprisoned by other men, concepts, or philosophies; we were created to be free.

If we are indeed going to live an unrestrained and uncontained life, I believe we must first have a solid understanding of God's original intention for the person He created us to be. Imagine with me for a moment, you just purchased a brand new digitally operated washing machine; feelings of excitement race through you as you load the machine, pour in the cleaning solution, and prepare to launch your first wash.

Suddenly you realize you have no idea how to operate this new, modern styled, voice-activated, digitally operated machine. Your mind is flooded with disappointment as you think to yourself, *"I have this wonderful machine, full of potential, but I do not know how to unlock it."* At that moment you remember, this machine came with an *operator's manual* provided by the manufacturer. You now realize that everything you need to know in order to unleash the power embedded in this machine is only a few page flips away.

Dear friend, I strongly believe our *real* freedom begins with an understanding that we were created by God—a Designer Original, full of purpose. Potential to prosper and succeed is woven within your DNA and is activated when you connect with the knowledge written in the operator's manual (the Bible) provided through your connection with the Creator.

The Creator's original plan for humanity was that we'd live in harmony through our connection with Him as a choice of our free will. Of course, separation entered in when mankind used their free will to choose a path forbidden by the Creator. This was the act that placed humanity in the most confining box of all. But God's love for His cherished creation moved Him to sanction the greatest escape from bondage ever known to man. Sending His own son to pay the penalty for mankind's free choice made it possible for all humanity to pass from the bondage of death to liberating life.

As long as we are willing to accept the sacrifice of God's son, Jesus, we can live life to the full as pronounced in scripture in John 8:36: *"If the Son, therefore shall make you free, ye shall be free indeed."*

Father, I present to you all who have read this book and have begun their ascent from the box that has confined them. I pray that the eyes of their heart will be flooded with the light of truth. The truth of who You are and who You have created them to be. I pray that each person reading this book will be strengthened, fortified, and assured that nothing is impossible for them as they place their trust in you.

Lead them and guide them into the understanding of the great treasure that is buried on the inside. Let them rise up and walk in the liberty that has been allotted to them. Finally, if they do not know You, I pray that You will reveal Yourself to them in a personal way. Overwhelm them with the power of Your love, so that they will accept You into their hearts as Lord and Savior in the matchless name of Jesus, The Christ, amen.

About the Author

Natalie B. Green is an author, speaker, personal mentor, and columnist, with a sincere desire to see people from all walks of life fulfill their God-given purpose. She possess a deep commitment to being a beacon of light and hope to hurting people everywhere.

In her role as co-pastor, she serves alongside her husband, Pastor James A. Green, Jr., at Heart of God Ministries Church, Inc., where she is the visionary and host of the life-changing women's fellowships, Unbroken Women's Encounter, as well as the Women of Purpose Fellowship and Conference.

A powerful, provocative, and energetic speaker for workshops, conferences, church functions, and women's events, Natalie garners the wisdom and insight acquired during her thirty-eight-year personal walk of faith. In addition, she is a columnist for the *Shulamite Women Community Magazine*, a magazine with a global reach. Natalie writes Devotionals under the sub-heading, *"Deeper Still."*

Natalie B. Green is devoted to her husband and daughter, Melody, and a doting Nana to Xavier, who has and will always be the first field of ministry for her.

CONTACT

Natalie B. Green

natalie@nataliebgreen.com

(786) 753-9309

www.nataliebgreen.com

- www.facebook.com/NatalieGreenMinistries
- www.twitter.com/NatalieBGreen
- www.linkedin.com/in/natalie-b-green-832a4332
- www.instagram.com/NatalieBGreen

www.ingramcontent.com/pod-product-compliance
Lightning Source LLC
Chambersburg PA
CBHW050607300426
44112CB00013B/2108